To

Sue Ann,

With Best!

Wishes

2016

# the boy
## who saved
## my life

He was two and a half, and everything came to a halt.
He stopped speaking. He wouldn't answer us.
He wouldn't look at us.

We were frightened.
We couldn't leave him alone and isolated in his world.
We were determined to fight for him.

As for me, I somehow knew I must open up myself to
him in a way I had never done with anyone. I had to
come out of my dark world to meet him in his world.
If I were going to help him, together we had to walk
hand in hand into the light of a better world.

I was haunted by the fear I didn't have enough in me
to give to him. I would come to know he had enough
in him to save my life, and rescue my soul.

**bright sky press**

2365 Rice Blvd., Suite 202 Houston, Texas 77005
Box 416, Albany, Texas 76430

ISBN 978-1-936474-01-1

10  9  8  7  6  5  4  3  2

Library of Congress Cataloging-in Publication Data on file with publisher.

Editorial Direction by Lucy Herring Chambers
Art Direction and Design by Ellen Peeples Cregan
Printed in Canada

# the boy who saved my life

### walking into the light with my autistic grandson

## EARLE MARTIN

Illustrations by Roxana Wieland

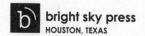
**bright sky press**
HOUSTON, TEXAS

Charlie looks up at me, and says,

> I don't know what I would
> do without myself.

Once again, I smile.
And I think to myself,
I don't know what I would do without him.

You may think the title of this book is astounding or overly dramatic, but the story behind it is rather simple. I have lived it. It is true. Because it is true for me and can be true for you, I hope you will read it.

In the following pages, I will tell you how Charlie saved me. I will share with you where I was when he appeared, and how he breathed life into me.

I think you will begin to develop a sense of what I am talking about. But I also think you will have more questions. How did all of this happen? And just who is Charlie?

I will try to answer your questions by telling you about our search for Charlie, who had become lost and whom we so desperately had to find. I will share stories with you so that you might know him better.

Then I will address you, for whom I am writing this book, and share how you might have your life profoundly changed— perhaps even saved—by your own Charlie.

Last, I will share my hopes for the future: for you, for me and for Charlie.

I hope you might read my words more than once. Reflect on them and ask what you might do after you set the book down.

Sincerely,

Earle Martin

*To Charlie, my best friend*

*~*

*To Charlie's mom,*
*Melinda.*
*Charlie, his dad Sam and I will tell you*
*she is* **"the best mom ever."**
*And as Charlie once said to Connie Hooper,*
*his high school teacher,*
**"She could be a doctor or a teacher or**
**anything else she wants to be,**
**you know, at home."**

*~*

*And, to your Charlie.*

## TABLE OF CONTENTS

## an introduction:

I ask you to begin here,
so you will understand
what comes after

THIS IS A STORY ABOUT CHARLIE. He is my grandson.
He is my best friend. This is a love story.

Charlie saved my life, and I want to share that with you.

I believe there is a Charlie waiting for you, waiting to be
your best friend.

Charlie has autism, and you will learn what he and his
family have done over these many years for him to be
the best he can be.

Charlie, to whom introductions are very important,
recently said to me,

> **I'm sorry that I
> didn't introduce you
> to myself earlier.**

I will introduce Charlie to you, and describe how both
he and I gave all we had to introduce each to the other.
Just so you know, early on he couldn't say "Pop" or "Pops,"
so I became "Pots." He would tell you,

> **My best friend in the
> whole wide world is Philip.**

Also his precious orange tabby cat, Annie.
But, as I said, Charlie is my best friend.

This is also a story about you and your Charlie, who can be
your best friend and change your life. Pause and think
about that. Your Charlie can be your best friend and change
your life. If you are like me, he or she can perhaps even save
your life.

My Charlie likes to say,

> **This is my lucky day!**

Knowing him makes everyday my lucky day. Finding your Charlie can be your lucky day.

With grave hesitancy, I share Charlie with you. His person. His character. His words. A priceless and yet vulnerable treasure. The way he reaches out and gives so much of himself. With an innocence and a pureness, yet without the rugged defenses you and I take for granted.

I must trust you not to hurt him, label him, nor mock his words. If that were to happen, I can't describe how sad I would be. Sad for you. Sad for me. And, most important, sad for Charlie.

When his little brother, Andrew, was seven or eight years old, he told me, "If anyone hurts my brother, I will put them in a room with snakes, cover them with boiling water, and shoot them." Well before Andrew knew Charlie had autism, he knew he had to look out for his older brother.

When he was thirteen, Charlie carefully looked at me and said,

> **Don't laugh at me.**

I couldn't stand your laughing at him. Rather, I invite you to enjoy him. And to smile, and even laugh, at his words. But let yours be a kind and joyful laughter.

About his words. He lost his language when he was two and a half, and didn't regain it until he was almost five. His words, cherished and carefully chosen, carry deep significance for him. He still works on them, saying,

> I want to get them just right. You know, just perfect.

What do I mean when I say, "He lost his language?"

As a toddler, Charlie was a child who talked. Then, without any warning, he just stopped talking. From time to time he could say isolated words, a word here, a word there, always with our strong prompting. But he really couldn't put words together. He couldn't say a sentence. He was without the ability to use his language, which most of us just take for granted. Would he ever be able to find it, to use it? We desperately hoped he would, all the while fearing he might not.

And then it happened. After two and a half years, just shy of his fifth birthday, it happened.

It was early on a Sunday morning, and Charlie had spent the night at our house. He and I walked down the stairs to have breakfast and watch a tape of one of his favorite children's television shows. And he fell. He wasn't hurt, just falling down a few carpeted steps. He got up, and turned toward me. He looked up at me, and said,

> **"Pots, Barney doesn't cry."**

He spoke. On his own, he spoke! He put two words together. He really put four words together! He found his language! He used his language. That was it, and he turned toward the kitchen. And I couldn't say anything.
I just cried.

He is fond of saying,

> **My two favorite words are 'absolutely delightful.'**

He continues,

> **I really like to say 'absolutely delightful.'**

For us, Charlie's words are just that. They remind us of the beautiful gift of language and brighten our lives.

If you have already found your Charlie, you will understand my reluctance—and joy—to share him. And if you find your Charlie later, you will know what I feel and what I mean.

I write these words from the deepest part of me, and I ask you to let them reach the deepest part of you.

Hold him well. Cherish him. Honor him.

As I said, Charlie has autism. A few words here might help you realize how being autistic is a profound and inescapable part of his life.

In his book, *Autism, Understanding The Disorder*, Dr. Gary Mesibov writes, "Today, we understand autism as a neurobiological condition that affects how people perceive and understand the world."

To me, that means Charlie's autism has radically changed the way his brain works. His brain is dramatically different from yours or mine. Because of those striking differences in his brain, he sees and reacts to the world in a different way than we do. He is thought to be high functioning, neither retarded nor as bright as many others considered higher functioning.

When Charlie was diagnosed in 1990, at the age of two and a half, we were told one in ten thousand children were diagnosed with an autism spectrum disorder. Figures publicized in 2009 from the CDC (Centers for Disease Control and Prevention) estimate that number had grown to one in one hundred and ten.

In her book *Thinking in Pictures,* Temple Grandin quotes Therese Joliffe's description of what reality is to an autistic person:

*Reality to an autistic person is a confusing inter-acting mass of events, people, places, sounds and sights. There seem to be no clear boundaries, order or meaning to anything. A large part of my life is spent just trying to work out the pattern behind everything. Set routines, times, particular routes and rituals all help to get order into an unbearable chaotic life.*

What you read in the following pages is not a definitive work about autism. It is my perspective and reflections on Charlie's autism, born out of our years of friendship. While you will glimpse some of what we have done to try to help Charlie deal with his autism—and his mom and dad far more than I—most of all I hope you will be able to grasp a sense of what he, himself, has accomplished. What we, together, have accomplished.

~

Over the years, we have come to realize Charlie will never be able to live alone. That truth was devastating when we first came to grips with it, and it will always be a grave concern. It is not the way it is supposed to be for your child, for your grandchild. And yet, having said that and knowing what it means, we believe he will be able to live with those who love him and whom he loves. We believe he will have a meaningful and happy life, and deepen the meaning and happiness of those around him. He has been doing that for years, and he does that now. Everyday.

I hope Charlie will be proud
should he ever read this book.

what comes next:

how Charlie
saved my life,
and rescued my soul.

WHEN CHARLIE STOPPED TALKING and stopped looking at us, when we were so afraid we might lose him to his own world, when we didn't know what to do next, something more profound than I had ever experienced began to awaken in me. Not only did I—alongside Melinda, his mother and my only daughter; Sam, his dad; and Katherine, Melinda's mother and my wife—have to explore every path to help him, but also I somehow knew I must open up myself to him in a way I had never done with anyone.

Always before, I held a certain amount of me back from others. It was the part I decided I couldn't give. What I needed to survive. I knew that holding back wouldn't work now. I had to give Charlie all I had. Without reservation. Afraid even that might not be enough to help him.

I was all the more desperately afraid I couldn't help him because this happened at a particular time in my life when I seriously questioned what I had to give. I knew I had to reach into me and try my best to reach into him, to share our worlds and meet each other. But when I looked into me, I wept. What I saw seemed so terribly wanting.

Charlie's grandmother, Katherine, whom he called Nanny, had been diagnosed in her late twenties with cancer. Although she was successfully treated, it left her with a fear she might not be able to raise our children. She went through years of a severe clinical depression. That was followed by more years of intense pain from rheumatoid arthritis. She fought these challenges valiantly. Yet the battle took a terrible toll. Charlie lifted her spirits in ways I had never before seen. Over and over she would play a greeting card recording of Charlie saying,

**"I love you, my Nanny."**

After he stopped talking, after he would no longer look at us, after we were afraid we might lose him, she wrote:

> *Charlie…My beloved little boy, so precious, so fair…Let me in, your world to share…You've always been your Nanny's boy—my very heart, my pride and joy! … You've brought me so much love and joy, and I want you to know, my little boy, that in that unseen "place" we meet—in our own and very special way, you are the love that lights my way.*

All Katherine had endured for so long had depressed me as well, even though at the time I wouldn't fully admit it to myself. I lived from one day to the next, functioning well enough to get by, in shades of gray and in stagnant air, in a kind of resigned sadness. Her suffering, in its own way, became my suffering. I felt sorry for her. Worse still, I felt sorry for myself. I had a life of more blessings than I ever dreamed of or deserved, yet I lived it without joy.

I had no desire to continue living, save to carry out my responsibilities. I endured. I felt inadequate. Laughter was a stranger. Beauty was hidden. As I looked inside of me, I couldn't find a life I wanted to live. As for my soul, my essence, my reason to be…I think I had forgotten about it. That deepest part of me had receded into the shadows. Except for my family, whom I loved, and those whom I counseled in my psychotherapy practice, to whom I was dedicated, I shut people out. I had given up on hope. For whatever reasons, I thought I would die within the next few years. That is simply how I felt.

Such was my life when I was suddenly overwhelmed with my desperate need to reach Charlie. To take his hand in mine. To offer him a hand worth taking. I understood that I must enter Charlie's world. I knew I had to come out of my dark world to meet him in his world. I knew that, together hand in hand, we had to walk out into the light of a better world.

And Charlie brought into my life the wonders of bright sunshine and fresh air. He gave me new life.
He rescued my soul.

How did he save my life? How did he rescue my soul?
How did he bring me out of my darkness? How I wish I
could somehow be with you now, for you to better grasp,
face to face, the absolute personal importance of what
I want you to know. To tell you personally what I believe
you can experience in your life.

My words and phrases can't begin to describe what Charlie
did, and still does, for me. But I ask you to give these words
special attention. Words like "honesty…truth…genuine…
joy…kindness…love." Phrases like "life- giving power…
a friendship beautiful just for itself…a new perspective…
he does his best to be the best he can be."

Pause and reflect on these words and phrases. You might
even meditate on them. You have heard them so often they
have perhaps lost any real meaning. It may be hard for you
to imagine they have substance. I realize it is asking a lot for
you to believe that I have chosen these words carefully and
that I believe them to be true. But that is what I ask.

~

The very first way Charlie saved my life was allowing us to be
genuinely together, each of us trying our best to be open to
the other. There I discovered the life-giving power of simply
being with him. The hours on end playing on the floor of
our dining room, now converted to a playroom for both
work and play. Both of us together on the floor. Both of us
together sitting side by side at the computer, delighting in

learning video games. Both of us together working at
our desk with our "In" and "Out" work boxes. Both of
us together reading story book after story book.
Both of us together sharing milk and cheese tacos.

Not sure Charlie could understand my words and knowing
he couldn't answer me, I would say, "Here I am, and I so
much want to know you, and want you to know me."
Knowing I wanted to know him, and fearing his knowing
me might not be enough to help him.

I wanted him to find in me a person no longer hiding in
the deep down shadows, a person to share a life with him
that I wasn't sure was even there. To realize and speak this
truth, and actually mean it, somehow let the first rays of
light into me. Not sure the me I felt myself to be could help
him, I discovered I could make myself a better me.

~

And then I discovered he liked me. Really. And he still
does. I did not like myself, but Charlie liked me. If you
have ever not liked yourself, you have a sense of what that
meant to me. In the beginning, and for such a long time,
he couldn't tell me that he liked me. But I felt it. I knew it.

Years later, a few months after Katherine died, he wrote,

> **If I won a million dollars,
> I would give the dollars to Pots.**

In response to an assignment to write five things that made him happy, number four was,

> " Having fun with Pots. "

I have those framed in my study. Not long ago he told me,

> " Pots, you are a kind old man. "

~

Being with Charlie, I came to realize that he wanted to share his life with me, to have me enjoy what he loved. We would sit side by side at the computer for hours on end, our heads only inches apart, his eyes constantly shifting between looking at the screen and looking at me. And when I would grow tired and close my eyes, before he found his language, he would gently reach over and raise my eyelids.

After he found his language, he would speak of our hours together as

> " A grandfather and grandson bonding time. "

I had not allowed myself to truly bond with someone for a very long time, and never with this sense of urgency and openness. While I have enjoyed friendships over the years, only now did I know what it really meant to have a best friend.

~

In spite of all he faced, he made himself happy. Being with him also made me happy, and then I started to make myself happy. I learned he was a far better person than I could ever have imagined him to be, and because of him I became a better person.

~

Increasingly I came to realize whatever Charlie faced in his life was much harder than anything I had known in my life. When he was younger we all did so much in his face. But now, with him intently in my face, I slowly allowed myself to look at how difficult his life would be. That humbling reality changed my perspective about my own life and the world around me. I discovered that a new perspective is an extraordinary gift, as I experienced fear and love both in sharp relief and in unexpected contrast to some of the more superficial realities of life to which I had become resigned.

To be with Charlie and to admire him as he has come so far in his quest to be all he can be has been a new experience for me. He inspires me, a rare gift. I can't say I have become all I can be, but I believe he has, and continues to do so. As he says,

> " I have patience and perseverance, and I never give up. "

~

Charlie is fond of saying,

> " I am on a mission. "

Before he and I began being together, I had not been on a mission for such a long time, and none like this. I entered into our mission with both anxiety and anticipation, not feeling that good about myself, unsure of what I had to give and afraid I would come up sadly lacking. With so much in the balance, I found being on such a vital mission to be a life-giving experience. I discovered I had life to give.

Once, as he was leaving our house, he said,

> **Goodbye, grandfather, I will not fail you. I will get the job done.**

He inspires me to do my job, even as I rejoice that I have a job to do.

~

Charlie has also given me the gift of someone to protect. With all he has accomplished and all of his efforts to be his best, he is still vulnerable in our world. He loves and cares, and is a delight to so many who know him, but he can never live alone. Taking together his level of abstract intelligence, language and lack of street smarts he will always need to be protected. He will always need to be shielded from injury or danger.

He once said to me,

> **Pots, I can't go on without you.**

The meaning of those words went far beyond the game we were playing. I am grateful to be one of the lucky ones who look out for him in ways he cannot do for himself. And I will do that for as long as I can.

~

Charlie has introduced me to a wondrous new world of exceptional boys and girls and men and women, each of whom has special needs. A dear friend of ours says, simply, each of them is "special." Innocent, vulnerable, holding their heads high in the face of unimaginable challenges, kind and giving, truly special people.

~

And he has introduced me to those who care about these exceptional people, share their frustrations and victories, give them love and are made the better because of this love between them. Had it not been for Charlie, I would never have known any of them.

~

Nor would I have come to know and love those remarkable men and women who have helped Charlie in so many ways, those whom we affectionately call Charlie's Angels. Being with them has also given me life.

Even as Charlie has prompted me to enjoy a sunrise, or smile when a fresh breeze crosses my face, he has also awakened me to want to engage people around me.

For years I had walked my neighborhood streets alone in the dark of early morning, head straight ahead, never looking at other walkers whom I passed. I am sure I had a stern look on my face, daring anyone to speak to me. Telling myself I needed that time to myself.

After being with Charlie for several years, I began to change. At first I credited that change to my closing my practice earlier than I had planned, in order to spend more time with Katherine. I told myself the change was because I missed the daily interactions with people in my practice. But then I realized it began before then. It began with Charlie.

I started smiling and introducing myself to everyone whom I met. Men and women whom I had silently passed for years, and anyone else I came across. And what would I talk about? Charlie, of course. These wonderful people came to know him as much as they knew me, and they would frequently ask about him.

IN YET ANOTHER WAY, HE HAS GIVEN ME LIFE
by my seeing what he has meant to others. How he has
brightened their lives. How he has brought them joy.
How he has transformed their vision of themselves and
their world around them.

Surely that is profoundly true for Melinda and Sam
and their family. For Charlie's godparents and friends.
For ever so many others who have come to know him.

HERE ARE THE WORDS OF JUST A FEW
WHOM HE HAS TOUCHED:

*…You've brought me so much love and joy, and I want you to know, my little boy, that in that unseen "place" we meet—in our own and very special way, you are the love that lights my way.*

Katherine
"My Nanny"

*Charlie changed my world and my life.*

Carol Selby
his teacher for six years

*What a special treat for us
to watch Charlie grow up
into such a delightful and
charming young man.*

Gary Mesibov
Director of Division TEACCH
University of North Carolina at
Chapel Hill

*Charlie is such a joy to be around.
He has a courageous spirit and
gentle soul. We are all so blessed to
be part of Charlie's world.*

*Charlie has taught me more
about teaching than any
university course could provide.*

Margaret Kroger
His teacher who now
lives in Australia

*We ALL love Charlie —
but for me especially, he
brightens my day and
keeps my priorities in line.*

Patti Stanwood
Manager of his
fitness center

*I've often thought about what
your dad said at our first
conference about how Charlie
"saved" his life. I just can't
tell you how very much I
enjoy Charlie. His humor (not
always on purpose but more so
now) just brightens my day.
He is a blessing to so many.*

Connie Hooper
His High School teacher
in a note to Melinda

*Early this morning, as we walked our three dogs, my husband and I saw the new moon high in the lightly bluing sky. The slightest sliver of silver embraced its front roundness as it hung suspended in space over the trees arched above us.*

*I thought of Charlie, who comes this afternoon. He is like that arc of silver, protecting riches inside, embracing growth still to come, yet fixed as a pure portion of a whole we will never completely know.*

Kristi
"My new grandmother."

And last, I believe Charlie has put me in touch with something deep within me. Perhaps it is what another dear friend calls the Charlie buried deep inside. Perhaps it is the little child in me, something long ago forgotten and covered over. Surely it is the life I had lost. The life he saved.

Perhaps it is my soul. That which I think is the very deepest part of me. I can't define it, but I am convinced it can be lost and it can be found. I believe Charlie has touched my soul, and in ways I think neither he nor I am fully aware, he has brought it out from the shadows and into the light.

Thank you, Charlie,
for saving my life.
Thank you for rescuing my soul.

I share our search
for Charlie:

he had become lost
and we so desperately
needed to find him

I ENTERED HIS HOME, TO WHICH I HAD A KEY. I was warmly greeted by Melinda. Andrew, his little brother, with a happy smile gave me a vigorous hug. Sam was at work. Max and Whitney, his older half brother and sister, were still at school.

And there he was. There was Charlie. Four years old, as handsome a boy as you would ever meet, he stood in the downstairs hall. He ran up to me, took my hand, and started to lead me to the front door.

Taking both of his hands, I stopped for a moment, and knelt down on one knee. Gently and firmly I faced him toward me. With a big smile, I looked at him right in the eye, and exclaimed, "Hi, Charlie! It's Pots! How are you?"

He never looked at me, and never said a word.

Instead, he tugged my hand, and I followed him to the front door.

Looking over my shoulder, I said goodbye to Melinda and Andrew, as Charlie pulled me to my car.

Once I buckled him in the back seat, we started the short four-block drive to my house. I adjusted the rear view mirror, so I could see his face. Quiet and composed, he was intent on where we were going.

We had driven this exact route hundreds of times in the past, down Wroxton Road to Hazard, left to Bissonnet, right to Woodhead, left to South Boulevard, and to our home on the southwest corner of South Boulevard and Dunlavy. He knew the way. We had taken it at least twice a week for most of his life.

I tried to change the route by just a block, right instead of left on Hazard, and he came apart. His face, calm and intent, broke into absolute terror. He became rigid. He poured tears. He made his loudest unhappy sounds, pointing to the direction I usually drive, demanding with all he had that I turn around. Demanding with all he had, except for words, for he had no words. He did not speak.

I stopped the car and turned around to face him, calmly telling him everything was all right, assuring him that we were going to our house. I explained I was just trying a different route, and we would soon be in our driveway.

Then I turned the car in the direction he knew and trusted. Slowly, he began to quiet, his tears stopped, and again he was intent on where we were going.

Persons who are autistic rely on routines for comfort and making sense of the world around them. Anything that deviates from a routine can be very scary. Each time I changed our route, Charlie became terribly upset. I still tried, hoping his reaction might be different. Hoping he might be able to tolerate the change. It was not to be the case that day. Not yet. Not for years to come.

We pulled to a stop in our driveway. I got out of the car, unbuckled him, and watched as he ran to our side door. He always ran. He ran fast. Then he stopped in front of the door, and shuffled his feet back and forth on the outside doormat. Over and over he shuffled his feet.

Each time he came to our door, he would shuffle his feet. I could never figure out why, and I'm still not sure. Perhaps it had something to do with being certain of where he was. Being certain it was safe to go inside. Perhaps it was a routine, to give him comfort.

He opened the door, and ran inside. Through the kitchen, and into the playroom. He went straight to a shelf with a stack of videotapes, selected one with "Sesame Street" segments which I had taped, and handed it to me to start playing. And he watched it, over and over, as he had done so many times before. Rather, we watched it, over and over, as we had done so many times before. Again and again. Again and again.

How I wished to know what was inside of him, what he thought, what he felt. But I didn't know. I just didn't know.

I had first met Charlie four years before in the delivery room of St. Luke's Episcopal Hospital in Houston, just blocks from his home. It was December 29, 1987. Melinda, who wanted to be a mom from the time she was a little girl and had already gone through a miscarriage, was holding her first child. Standing beside them were Sam and Katherine. It was a time of joy and gladness.

We joyfully embraced him. I thought he was a beautiful baby, and was nervous holding him for even a short time. A large framed photograph of him and his mom, taken the day after his birth, hangs above me as I write now. I smile when I look at it, and what I see is pure grace.

Charlie came into a warm and welcoming home, where he would be deeply loved and adored. And how he would be hugged! Soon he would spend the night with us, and Katherine would rock and sing to him hours on end. And, again, how he was hugged! He was my first grandson, and of course I loved him, but not with the depth of Katherine's love.

Once, before we had lost him, I was sitting next to him in his highchair in the playroom watching "Sesame Street." I wandered a few feet into the kitchen to take a break. Katherine appeared, "When he is in there, you are not to be in here. You are to be in there with him!" In her direct and plainspoken way she really introduced me to Charlie, and for that I will always be grateful.

He grew and seemed to flourish, drawing admiration for what he appeared to learn at such a young age. We all thought he was precocious. At twenty months, he knew his ABC's, 123's, and shapes. He could say a word for each letter of the alphabet. He read numbers and letters on billboards and license plates, and was skilled with puzzles. He memorized board books, learned how to use a VCR, and started developing his Nintendo skills. He learned to walk on his own, never letting us hold his hands to help him.

We experienced Charlie as a sweet and loving child who seemed to enjoy giving his head and body to be kissed and hugged by his family, especially by Melinda and Katherine.

Yet we were not without concerns. About the time he turned two, he was with thirty or so children at a gymnastics birthday party for a three-year-old little girl. The instructor told the children to assemble and follow him around the gym. Except for three or four children who didn't want to leave their mothers, all of the boys and girls formed a line. But not Charlie. He walked by himself to the middle of the gym, played with random pieces of equipment, lay down and, pivoting on his stomach, smiled as he watched the other children follow their instructor in a circle around him. One of the mothers, who is also Andrew's godmother, later said to Melinda, "I think Charlie just marches to a different drummer!"

We thought he was cute and funny, and that this was yet
another example of his independence and stubbornness.
We marveled at what he could do, and played down his
differences from others his age. Those might be
developmental delays, and would be resolved in time.
We had our concerns, but we thought he would turn
out to be "normal," whatever that might be.

~

When Charlie was two and a half, everything came to
a halt. Not everything, but that's the way it felt to us.
Melinda and Katherine caught it right away. He no longer
responded to our talking to him. He didn't answer us.
He didn't turn his head toward us. He didn't look at us
in the eye. A fire engine, siren wailing, raced by him
and Melinda as they played in their front yard.
He never looked up. He never turned his head.

Thinking he might be deaf, we had his hearing checked at
Texas Children's Hospital. We discovered he could hear.

What was it? Had you been with us, you would have seen
our absolute fear. And you would have seen something else:
Melinda's loving determination. This was her Charlie, and
she would do everything she could to help him.

He was soon diagnosed with something called PDD/NOS,
which stands for Pervasive Developmental Disorder/Not
Otherwise Specified. Autism is the largest and most

pronounced form of the pervasive developmental disorders, but we were told that what he had was probably not autism itself. They really didn't know what it was, but it probably wasn't autism. Did I just repeat that? Yes, and we repeated it as long as we could. We knew little about autism, but it frightened us.

We were told he might grow up to be awkward, a geek, a nerd. He might be a rocket scientist. He would have some problems with social interactions, but he could still have a bright future. Those hopes were tentative at best, but we held on to them as long as we could.

However, still thinking it was not autism itself, we were told later if he didn't get his language by the time he was five, he might never have it. That fear burned deep within us, making it all the more difficult to hold onto our hopes.

~

We believed our search for Charlie should begin with his diagnosis and how to deal with it. Find out what he was facing and then find him—which meant exploring what appeared to us a mysterious maze of pervasive developmental disorders and where he might be within it. Like parents and grandparents before and after us, we searched for answers everywhere we could.

We worked with a psychologist, which included session after session on the floor of his office with Charlie. Doing simple things, like building blocks and playing with toy cars. Always with tiny, discrete steps in sequence. Over and over. Always in Charlie's face. Encouraging him and, when that didn't work, trying to force him to participate. Day after day, week after week, month after month. Whatever we did there, Melinda repeated at home, over and over on her own, always in his face, determined to cure him.

Before going into the office for the floor sessions, Charlie would lose himself in the long drapes of the waiting room. Perhaps he was just passing the time or exploring, or maybe he was hiding from the hour he was about to endure. In time, I realized it was more than that. It was something that has proved invaluable for him, his need to be alone, to have time to himself. His quiet time.

I also learned something else about Charlie. Along with his independence and stubbornness, I discovered another quality: he would always try to do his best. Although we encouraged, prodded and demanded so much of him, we sensed he was doing all he could to reach out to us. He must have had to dig deep down, and it took a very long time, but he did it.

Much later, long after he found his language again, looking back on what he must have experienced as endless years of our imposing so much on him, he told Melinda,

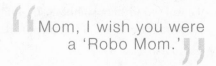

Mom, I wish you were a 'Robo Mom.'

She asked what that meant, to which he replied,

> **Then you would do what I tell you to do.**

We fought so he could use his language. But on a much more significant and profound level, we fought for him. We did all we knew to find Charlie. So he would not be left alone and isolated in his world. We fought to enter his world, and for him to enter our world. Only later would I look back and realize how hard he fought side by side with us.

We took him to multiple therapies, five days a week. In our first of countless sessions of speech therapy, he would sit at a small table across from the therapist, with Melinda and me sitting beside him. Like any little boy, he was given toy cars to play with, but with a profound difference at this table. Here he was constantly told, "Talk it! Talk it! Charlie, talk it!"

There was progress. Facing us, with our hands on his shoulders and our eyes looking right into his, he would repeat after us, "Hi," and "Goodbye." In time, he would repeat the last word or words of a sentence or a phrase we said to him, which we learned was called "echolalia." We tried to get him to say, even with just one word, what he wanted.

I remember a day when Melinda, holding Charlie tight in her arms, and I were racing across the emergency room at Texas Children's Hospital to meet a plastic surgeon for a deep cut on Charlie's chin. Every time we passed a nurse or a tech, Melinda would stop and ask his or her name. Say it was a woman whose name was Sally. Melinda would look at Charlie, whom she was holding in her arms, and say to him, "Charlie, say 'Hi, Sally.'" He would repeat,

" Hi, Sally. "

Melinda did this to give him a routine in a frightening situation, to comfort him, to help him feel safe.

~

In March of 1991, when he was three, we took Charlie to the Yale Child Study Center in New Haven, for a second opinion. There we had to find our way down what seemed an endless series of long hallways to the room in which he would be evaluated. The following day, not remembering how to find the same room, we were ready to again ask directions. But we never did. We didn't have to. Instead, Charlie led us as he ran down the never-ending maze of hallways to the exact room where we had been the day before.

Fred Volkmar, the director of the Center, gave us the same diagnosis we had received before: PDD/NOS, related to autism, but not autism itself. He said this was probably what Charlie had, but it was too soon to be sure.

One more thing about Charlie emerged in that visit. It is often said that autistic children are not affectionate, but with Charlie that wasn't true. Even though he wouldn't look at us in the eye, he readily let us hug him. We were told it might be because he had been so constantly hugged by Melinda and Katherine from the day he was born.

~

In August of that year, Melinda and I drove out to Brookwood, a community for functionally challenged adults, about twenty miles from Houston. It is described as "an exciting, God-centered community of people with unique needs and abilities finding and sharing better ways to live, learn, work and play."

I could fill a book with the wonders of that beautiful place, but our aim on this trip was to visit with Yvonne Streit, who, with her husband, Dave, was inspired by their daughter, Vicki, to start both Brookwood and, before that, the Briarwood School.

Briarwood is a school where most of the students have learning differences. The other students, like Charlie, have developmental delays. They are in Briarwood's Special

School, named the Tuttle School. A guiding principle for all of Briarwood is,

> **"We believe every child can learn and every child has the right to be taught in the way that he or she learns best."**

I knew Vicki had suffered brain damage from complications resulting from mumps at an early age. What neither Melinda nor I knew then was that Yvonne also had a grandson who would years later become Charlie's friend and whom Charlie would join in the Tuttle School at Briarwood and later at Brookwood.

Yvonne told us what works with one child may not work with another, and whatever we did, it was best not to try to make them into little robots. She said hugging and other positive physical contact was essential, and Charlie likely wouldn't be in as good a place as he was without all of the hugging and affection from the day of his birth.

That day Yvonne told Melinda that in the many years ahead, she would be many things for Charlie. She would play many different roles. Teacher. Therapist. Nurse. And so many more. But Yvonne's most poignant words, words that still bring tears to Melinda were these: "Never forget, first and foremost, you are his mother."

~

In October of 1992, we met Arnold Miller and Eileen Eller-Miller, who had worked for twenty five years with children like Charlie. I had read their book, *From Ritual to Repertoire*, and invited them to come to Houston. They came, and the following May, Melinda took Charlie to their center in Boston.

They gave us useful suggestions on ways for Charlie to both expand his world and adapt to our world. They taught us how to help him become aware of himself, to form an identity. They encouraged us to talk face-to-face with Charlie about himself. We talked to him about him. We wrote stories about him for him to read. I put mirrors on every vacant wall in our dining room, now turned into a play room, so he would see himself wherever he looked. (He still likes to look in the mirror.) We used our own limited version of the Millers' elevated platforms, on which he had to make his way carefully to the other side without falling, to help him gain a greater awareness of himself and the world around him.

We used their "symbols accentuation program," a video program which takes figures (dogs, cats, people, whatever) and changes them into letters, much like what we had watched on "Sesame Street." Melinda believes this program, which is still available today, did more than anything else to teach Charlie how to read.

We learned from them how to transition Charlie from one activity to the next, the importance of which I can't overstate. Melinda has shared their counsel with others, which has proven successful.

Charlie, even at his very young age, was a whiz at Nintendo, but he strongly resisted our trying to get him to leave it for something else. The Millers taught us that all we had to do was to tell him he was going to do another activity for a certain time period and then could return to his Nintendo. They advised us to tell him twenty minutes ahead of time before he would leave his Nintendo, after which he could return to it. We then repeated that in five minute intervals. Finally, we told him it was time to change. We tried their advice, and it worked.

The Millers recognized how Melinda's intense work with Charlie had taken a toll on them both, and they suggested she ease off somewhat. Rather than put on her work hat each time she sat down to do therapy with him, they recommended she see therapy as a special kind of play time, in which she was better able to follow what he was doing and learn more about him. Begin where he was, slowly lead him to new things, all without upsetting him too much. He had significant problems, but most importantly he was an adorable little boy whom Melinda needed to enjoy.

Even more valuable to us than receiving their excellent practical suggestions, we also learned what we instinctively knew, what we desperately wanted, but had all too often become obscured to us. We learned anew to value Charlie's person, and to help him discover himself as we discovered him. We needed to remember finding him was our primary goal. To better understand his needs, to help him develop himself, and to respect and enjoy him.

I subscribed to a publication called *The MAAP*, which stands for "Families of More Advanced Individuals with Autism, Asperger's Syndrome, and Pervasive Developmental Disorders/Not Otherwise Specified." Susan Moreno, the editor, always closes each issue with the cherished words, "You are not alone."

I read about something called Division TEACCH, which stands for **T**reatment and **E**ducation of **A**utistic and related **C**ommunication-handicapped **C**hildren, part of the University of North Carolina at Chapel Hill. The first part of its mission statement is "To enable individuals with autism to function as meaningfully and independently as possible in the community." I started corresponding with its director, Gary Mesibov.

I told Melinda about Gary, and she said, "I'll call him and ask him to come to Houston." She called him, and he came. As Charlie likes to say,

"Simple as that."

He and a delightful colleague, Kaia Mates, arrived in Houston in February of 1994. Charlie was now six years old. It had been about three and half years from the day he wouldn't look at us and lost his language, and a little more than a year from the morning he fell down our steps, looked at me and said,

"Barney doesn't cry."

By that time Charlie had spent two years at The Westview School, then a pre-kindergarten. While it now goes through middle school and is just for children with autism spectrum disorders, it was at that time an amazing mix of primarily autistic and Downs children together with those who had other functional disabilities. At this point he had moved on to a Montessori kindergarten. We discovered Maria Montessori founded her school for children not unlike Charlie. He was the only special needs student in the kindergarten class, and there he had happily bonded with a pet bunny.

Gary and Kaia liked Montessori, having found it to be child-centered, visual, quiet and structured. I remember looking in at them through an outside window, just quietly sitting in the classroom, hardly noticed, as they carefully watched Charlie.

They observed Charlie in his home, fitting gently and comfortably into his family, somehow like old friends. They had long discussions with Melinda, Sam and me.

"What do you think?" we at last asked. "Well, he is autistic," said Gary. "Charlie has autism." Gary confirmed what we had long feared. But by now knew what we had been so afraid of was. We were not surprised, because all the signs we saw in him pointed to that diagnosis. We could now face it squarely, most of all because we trusted Gary and believed he would help Charlie and help us. Gary has been our touchstone ever since, and we have never been disappointed.

Gary later wrote, "We don't want to discourage your efforts in any way. On the other hand, as we discussed, Charlie is not only autistic but he's a child as well and you must remember to cultivate that child side from time to time. Our suggestion is to continue your impressive work but give yourself and Charlie many well deserved breaks."

Melinda took Charlie to Chapel Hill for his first evaluation in 1996. Sitting in Gary's office, she began to cry. She told him if she took a moment to relax, read a newspaper or have a cup of coffee, she felt she was giving up on Charlie, giving up on trying to cure him. Gary responded that Charlie needed to be as happy as he could be so that he could be more receptive to learning. When she left his office, she felt deep down he had given her permission to relax and to be Charlie's mom—to enjoy him—and for him to be her little boy.

More times than I can remember, we have written, called and emailed Gary with all manner of questions and concerns, always receiving quick and helpful answers, often sent at five or six in the morning. While it wasn't the most important thing he helped us with, I enjoyed his response when we asked about Charlie's fear of the dark. Gary's thoughts, among other things, included the suggestion to have Charlie eat a donut in the dark!

Once I wrote Gary that Charlie, who loved playing his Nintendo games, would become absolutely inconsolable if he couldn't accomplish every goal. Both then and now

Charlie would say,

**"I never give up."**

I had tried everything, without success, to help him not get so upset. Gary said people with autism rely heavily on the visual, on what is written down. He suggested I simply write that Charlie could be a good player without accomplishing all of his goals, and give it to him. The next day, driving him to our house from school, I gave him what I had written. He read it silently—more than once, I think—and handed it back to me. I asked whether or not he wanted to talk about it, but he remained quiet.

That day at our house, after he had completed the work I had planned, he went to play his Nintendo. But with a profound difference. He didn't complete all of his goals, but for the first time he didn't get terribly upset. He handled his occasional frustrations well, playing his games with joy. Gary's suggestion proved right.

Following that experience, on countless occasions I would write and Charlie would read. The results were worthwhile, though not without reservations on his part. One day he came into our house, looked at the paper laid on the desk before him, and said,

**"Pots, enough of your writings!"**

Several months later, he said,

> Pots, I know you don't want to hear this, but I don't like your house at write time.

By then he meant not only my writings, but his writings as well, which I increasingly insisted he do.

About the time he entered puberty, he had his first seizure. We were at his family's lake house. The seizure lasted for about three minutes, followed by forty-five minutes of deep sleep, and another two and a half hours of drowsiness. All he could tell us was he had experienced "a horrible thought."

We immediately called Gary, who told us it was absolutely critical we make an appointment as soon as possible with a pediatric neurologist for a full work-up. Continuing seizures, especially if they were severe, could be devastating.

At Texas Children's Hospital, we were told Charlie had experienced a complex partial seizure, somewhere between a petit and grand mall. When Melinda told Charlie they were going to the pharmacy for medicine so he might not have more horrible thoughts, he replied,

> A cure!

We also learned that about twenty percent of autistic children entering puberty begin having seizures, which can continue into their adulthood.

Charlie has experienced more seizures over the years, each milder than the first, and while his medication has increased, he has been extraordinarily fortunate that he has not experienced any noticeable side effects. Recently, when his neurologist prescribed he wear an EEG monitoring device for forty-eight hours to check his brain waves, complete with numerous wires attached to his head and body, Charlie told everyone,

> I am Wire Sponge.

When I asked, he reminded me that Wire Sponge is a Megaman Nintendo character.

I wrote of Gary Mesibov, "In the midst of a world of some-times-loud voices and claims, his is a calm voice, and his only claim is that he wants to help both Charlie and us."

And here is what Gary wrote about Charlie following his last evaluation: "What a special treat for us to watch Charlie grow up into such a delightful and charming young man whose continued progress is a clear reflection of the strong team of support spearheaded by his family and enhanced by his school program."

Our search for Charlie was framed by his having autism. We felt the more we knew about his autism the more we might know about him. Perhaps we might even come to know him, for that was always our aim.

About Charlie's own awareness of his autism, we really don't know. He has only asked about it once, years ago, and Melinda told him it was something that made him very special. From time to time since then, he has said,

> I am special.

But he might say,

> I am special because I have two webbed toes.

He is also fond of saying,

> I am special because of Annie, my cat.

He is aware of a book I wrote, *Dear Charlie*, which says on the cover it is a guide for his living his life with autism, although he has never read it. Once he told Melinda,

> My teacher has a copy of *Dear Charlie* on her desk.

Knowing he had never even asked about the book, she
asked whether or not he knew what the book was about.
He replied,

> Yes. It's the story of my life.

Once in class, when the subject of autism came up,
he volunteered,

> Autism is a different
> way of thinking.

We don't know whether or not he really grasped what he
was saying, or what meaning it might have for him.
On another occasion he said to me,

> Pots, I am different.

When I asked how he might be different, he replied,

> Maybe I don't
> have my strategy.

He immediately moved on to something else, and I did not press him any further. But I found it telling, because he frequently speaks of his Nintendo characters needing their strategy in order to be successful.

Unless he brings it up related to something concrete, such as his being caused hurt or anxiety, Gary recommends we don't bring his autism up to him. It would be too abstract for him, and would likely just cause him worry without giving him understanding.

Before I describe who we found him to be, his person and his character, I want to underscore that this wasn't just our search. It was also Charlie's search both for himself and for us. As I mentioned earlier, he likes to say,

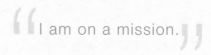

"I am on a mission."

We are convinced he has been on a mission, and we will never be able to imagine how hard he has worked.
And we believe he has been successful in his mission.

In July of 2007, Melinda, Charlie and I were at an airport terminal magazine store. He had gone around the corner. Not seeing him, Melinda called, "Charlie!"

"Yes.

he answered,

"What is it?

"I just wanted to find you," she replied.

"Mom, I am as found as I can be,

said he.

We found him.

And he found us.

Let me tell you
more about Charlie:

I shall speak as I might if
you and I were together

BECAUSE CHARLIE, WHOM WE WERE AFRAID we might never find, means so much to us, I have searched for the best way to help you know him. I will try to paint a montage of images of Charlie, using words as the paint from my brush. As you might describe someone dear to you.

We often tell "Charlie Stories." They are brought to mind by one of us asking the other, "Do you remember when...?"

I share with you here only a few of our stories, but I hope enough to give you a feeling for his person and his character.

You will glimpse his always trying his best. His responding to adversity. And his reaching out and caring for others. You will experience his values and priorities. And you will discover he likes himself, an accomplishment that is at once difficult, beautiful and profound.

Within the formidable parameters presented by his autism, Charlie tries as hard as he can to do his best. He really does, which is a beautiful thing to see. Simply put, that is his quest. In spite of his being afraid, he presses ahead, saying

"I am brave...I never give up."

It was the fall of 2000, and Charlie was then thirteen. He, Melinda and I were driving to an old gym near downtown Houston. Old homes on old leafy streets, a warm, pleasant evening. It was his introduction to Special Olympics basketball, and he was scared to death. Not only was it something new, which is especially hard for someone with autism, there was more:

> **I am scared. I don't know if I can play by their rules. I can play by my rules. But I don't know if I can play by their rules.**

His rules consisted of a script which he wrote in his head, with roles assigned to him and me, which we played out on afternoons on our back driveway. But now he would have to play by the rules of basketball, albeit somewhat relaxed. He couldn't call the shots. He couldn't assign roles. He couldn't control the outcome.

He soon overcame his fear, learned to play by the new rules, made some good shots, passed the ball, defended his goal and loved it.

> **Pots, I've learned the rules of basketball! I can play basketball!**

After his second year of rock climbing at a gym with his
Briarwood School classmates he wrote,

> I wish my family could see how
> high I can climb. Rock climbing is hard
> work for me. When I climb three times,
> my arms get tired. I am proud of myself
> when I make it to the top.

Sam was with him for another climb at a Boy Scout climbing
wall, and he wrote,

> It was a bonding time with
> my father and me. You know,
> a father and son bonding time.

On that occasion, while preparing to ascend the wall,
he turned to Sam, smiled, and said,

> Dad, you know that box of
> magazines under my bed? If anything
> happens to me, get rid of it.

There was no box of magazines, of course; it was just a line
he learned from a children's movie, *Dunstan Checks In.*
It cracked Sam up. One line among many others he learned
from his recorded videos, movies and games, internalized
in part because he could play them over and over. You can
imagine the broad smiles from those standing nearby.

Charlie works hard to say his words in just the right way, perhaps because he lost his language and to find it means so much to him. When he takes a long time to be satisfied with saying a sentence, he sometimes says,

> "Maybe it's taking me a long time to say it right because I'm getting old like you, Pots."

Part of his autism is being a perfectionist, and most likely that contributes to the frequency with which he uses his words,

> "Just right. You know, Pots, just perfect."

He might begin a sentence fifteen or twenty times, trying to master just the right pronunciation, the right tone, the right pitch and with the right affect.

~

Sometimes he lets up on himself, saying,

> "I don't have to be perfect."

He might say,

> When I play my Nintendo games on easy, which I like best, I have to be perfect. I don't have to be perfect on medium or hard.

After correctly guessing the answer to a question on *Jeopardy*, which he loves, he told me,

> I guessed William Henry Harrison, but I changed my mind, to Andrew Jackson. I was lucky.

Following an hour of frustration in accomplishing a goal he looked at me,

> Pots, I'm going to try something new, a sense of humor. What is a sense of humor?

After I replied it was laughing at what was bothering him, he smiled,

> Oh, I get it. The laughing thing, that's it.

And Charlie has been able to say, although not often,

> I can say, 'I failed. I made a mistake. It was my fault.'

He was on the dais for the second time at a Special
Olympics track meet, and the announcer said,
"Here is Charlie Stubbs for his second gold medal.
He really likes to talk!"

To which Charlie, who had lost his language for two and
half years, smiled and replied,

> **Talking is my favorite pastime.**

His heart is set on winning the gold medal, countering all
of my efforts to persuade him that's not so important,

> **Pots, I don't have time to play these
> games with you. I need the money!**

He keeps all of his gold medals hanging in his room, while
the silver and bronze hang in his parents' room. And yet, as
he has matured over the years, I think he really grasps the
motto of Special Olympics:

*Let me win,
but if I cannot win,
let me be brave in the attempt.*

Another window into Charlie is his way of dealing with adversity, his reactions to a life full of frustrations.

Like most of us, he wants to put them aside when he can. During his birthday party at the aquarium we overheard him hesitantly saying to his teacher,

> **Do we have to talk about the 'consequences?'**

~

If he has gotten into trouble, he might say,

> **I never talk about disgrace stories.**

When he can't hide his tears or the anguish in his face over something which made him sad, he might say,

> **It's such a long story, I don't want to talk about it.**

However, if we show patience and encouragement he will talk about it, for which we are grateful. He has written these things that make him sad:

> **Detention, losing a sport, name calling, laughing at me and cross voices.**

Sometimes he works things out on his own, without talking about what has given him grief. Following a sad day at school, which Melinda suggested I not pursue with him, he arrived to spend the night. He quietly greeted the dogs,

> Hi puppies, I'm home. Hi Nimrod. Hi Muffin. Hi Ouisie. I'm home.

With a subdued voice, he greeted Kristi and me,

> Hi Kristi. Hi Pots. I'm home.

The next morning, Kristi fixed him breakfast.

> Thank you, Kristi, for breakfast. For the two eggs over easy, the bacon, the skim milk, the hot cocoa and the no pulp orange juice. I really liked that round bacon. Do you call that 'Canadian bacon?' Thanks Kristi, for the best breakfast ever! You gave me protein and hot cocoa. That will make me strong, and ready for PE today.

And he concluded,

> Well, blow me down, and shiver me timbers, it's turned out to be a good Charlie day after all.

Once he told me,

" Pots, when your heart
is broken, go to a church.
A church is a good place to go.
Like your church,
Christ Church Cathedral.
Or Chapelwood Church.
Or any church.
For a little peace and quiet. "

Not infrequently he will join his hands together in a prayer
position, looking up and down as he composes himself, and
meditate

" for calm and control. "

Recently he was upset with two classmates on the playing field, and retreated into his classroom to be alone. There he was surprised to discover Connie Hooper, his incredibly gifted high school teacher. She asked him to talk about his sadness, and they worked the problem through. She also suggested he come up with a code word he could say to her when other students were around and he didn't want them to know he was unhappy. He thought for a minute, and came up with "P and Q." When she asked what that meant, he replied,

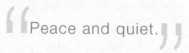
Peace and quiet.

When he plays basketball, he will say,

> I have to get baskets to cheer me up.

In a particularly tough game, he told us,

> I need family. I need support.

In another game, he fell to the floor. We made ourselves wait in the stands, waiting to see how he handled it. Then he said, loud enough for all to hear,

> Will someone from the Stubbs family come down here!

It turned out he had broken his finger, and we drove to the hospital emergency room. As we passed a drugstore, he said,

> I hope I will get well soon. Should we stop to buy a 'get well' card?

When he was later told his finger would always be a little bent, he commented,

> My finger will be bent for eternity.

Connie has taught Charlie and his classmates to stand up for themselves, and he does that. However, he has also learned when it is time to back down. Then he is quiet,

> But in my mind I talk to the other person. I know I am right, but I say it only in my mind. Sometimes I play mind games when I am angry at someone. And I don't get too close to them.

~

In a student-teacher basketball game, Charlie was reprimanded for something he said. He was sidelined for ten minutes and told to write an apology. He did as he was told, but he then put a towel over his face so no one could see him crying. He arrived at our house, sad as he could be, asking for a dish towel to put over his face,

> It's like what some women wear to church, to hide their faces.

He got a large paper sack from the pantry, asking me to cut places for his eyes, nose and mouth. With the sack on his head, he said,

> Now I can keep my face alive.

After I suggested wearing the paper sack might draw more attention to him, he removed it and we talked and ate potato chips.

The next day Charlie had a scheduled appointment with the orthodontist, and asked Melinda for permission to go inside the office alone. He later emerged with an order for a mouth guard. On his own, he had come up with a solution for a problem which had caused him so much grief.

> I will wear it when I play basketball, or any sport, and it will keep me from saying bad things.

The following day he told me,

> It will help me keep my mouth shut. And I think it is a crafty touch. I learned it from Weldar, in 'Banjo Tooie'.

If, unlike me, you have not watched the Nintendo *Banjo Tooie* dozens of times, you should know Weldar is a villain who becomes a good guy.

In August of 2009, his beloved Annie died, his orange tabby cat who had been with him through thick and thin for nine years, sitting in his lap and sleeping beside him in his bed.

> **"Annie is now in heaven with Muffin and Sassy and Steve...and so many, many people and dogs and cats, you name it! She was my whole life. How nice she is on my mouse pad, and I can see her picture when I play my games."**

And he continued,

> **"Mom and I made cookies, to cheer me up."**

Around his seventeenth birthday, Charlie wrote a letter which he saved on the computer as "Charlie's blues letter." He had gotten upset with four people at school the day before, and Melinda, remembering Gary's suggestion, encouraged him to write down what was bothering him.

These are the four people I'm upset with.

Ms. Hooper…she got me into a tiny bit of trouble and I was worried that she would write down something no good for me which is even worse because she thinks I am guilty and I don't want to fall for that again because that will break my heart….

Mrs. Baker…I was trying to get to my space but Mrs. Baker said "No" because Joanna and Tom were there and I heard they go to random places and even when they get to my place that breaks my heart too and I did not like that at all.

Matthew…even when he knows everything I'm going to do, Matthew on any base would just run to the next base and he would sometimes try to taunt me and that can break my heart too….

Bill…Last Friday, when P.E. was over, we put the heavy mats up. Bill was with me putting a mat up but when he was about to put the mat up, he just ran out on me and it can break my heart too.

And those are the four things that broke my heart which I call a quadruple broken heart.

P.S. If I get a quintuple broken heart, I would pretend to faint.

Thank you!
Charlie Stubbs

Charlie reaches out to others. He cares for others. His trying to connect with them and giving himself to them reveals another dear part of him.

~

Charlie had completed his kindergarten year, and we searched for a Montessori elementary school. Following one frustration after another, we finally found Alief-Westwood Montessori School. We met Carol Selby, its talented director, who would become his teacher from first through sixth grades.

As we observed the other children in their classroom to determine if it would be a good placement for him, we told her we didn't think he could do what would be asked of him. We also told her he couldn't do math, because Montessori teaches math using beads, and at his former school he was afraid of the beads.

As to the beads, she said, "We'll see." As to our concerns that he couldn't do what would be asked of him, she explained to us, "Someone has to take the chalk to the blackboard. Some-one has to wipe it clean. Someone has to get the books from the shelves." We listened to her, and we saw her enthusiastic and authoritative smile. At that moment, we knew this was the right school for Charlie.

Carol constantly set up situations for him to succeed. She began by having him pat the younger children to sleep at nap time, giving him a sense of responsibility for someone else. Then she showed him the exact same kind of math beads he was afraid of, and he told her he couldn't use them.

She replied, "These are my beads, and they are different."

He began to use the beads. Two years later he graded the other students' math tests, signing each paper and making notations like

"Great job."

or

"Great work."

or

"You missed this one. Better luck next time."

~

Winning a Special Olympics gold medal takes on exceptional significance when it comes to Bocce Ball, because Charlie considers it his best sport. He is fond of saying,

"I am a Bocce Ball master."

So when he was asked whether or not he would agree to be paired with Philip, who was not as adept at Bocce Ball as Charlie, we wondered how he would respond to his dilemma. The gold or possibly not. The answer came quickly,

> **I will play with Philip, my best friend in the whole wide world.**

They did play together, and it was a beautiful sight to behold.

They also won the gold medal.

~

I think of a photograph of Jane Stewart, the first teacher Charlie had when he was three, kneeling in front of him, looking at him square in his face, holding his shoulders firmly, and saying, "Look at me. Charlie, look at me." I am reminded of the hundreds, if not thousands of times we have done the same with him. And of the countless times Melinda told him to say "Hi" to whomever they would meet.

Now, wanting me to be very much involved with him and his enjoyment of what he is doing, he tells me

> **Pots, look at me. I need your eyes. Look at me...about this attention thing... pay attention, Pots...I need you to talk to me, Pots....**

Now he introduces himself to everyone he meets, intently looking them in the eye,

> **Hi, I'm Charlie Stubbs.
> What's your name?**

He loves what he calls the "introductions," and he will tell me,

> **Pots, it's fun to introduce yourself.**

We were on a plane headed for London, and he'd made friends with someone across the aisle from him, a woman whose name was Charlotte. When the lights went out and the passengers were closing their eyes, he called out,

> **Goodnight Charlotte.
> Have a good sleep.**

She looked over at me, a big smile on her face, "Goodnight Charlie. Have a good sleep."

Recently we were in a restaurant, and Charlie, now twenty-one, asked for permission to go to the bar. He didn't order anything to drink, and if he had, it would have been milk, but he stayed until we ate dinner, and then returned to the bar after dinner. As we left, we found him in his bright smiley T shirt sitting with five adults having a wonderful time. He introduced us to each of them, and told us

> **I have been rapping around with my friends.**

It turned out that one of them works with autistic children and another has an autistic son. They laughed and told us they had thoroughly enjoyed their visit with Charlie. Later he told Melinda,

> **See, mom, I make friends wherever I go.**

Several years earlier Charlie, Kristi and I were enjoying a picnic at a park near our home. Close by, a group of older boys, looking tough and street smart, were playing basketball. In spite of our caution, he said,

" It's alright. "

and walked over to them.

" Hi, teenagers, I'm Charlie Stubbs. "

He asked if he could join in, and one of the boys tossed him the ball. He made a shot, played with them for about five minutes, and handed back the ball,

" Thanks, gang. "

Returning to us, he said,

" That's the gang. "

One of my fondest memories in that park was when a young mother and her little boy sat down near where Charlie and I were having our picnic. I noticed she had a serious, even worried look on her face, never once smiling. Then came his introduction,

> Hi, I'm Charlie Stubbs.
> This is my grandfather, Pots Martin.
> His real name is Earle Martin.
> His first wife was Nanny,
> who passed away unexpectedly.
> His second wife is my
> new grandmother, Kristi.

As you might imagine, she smiled and then laughed.
And the four of us enjoyed a few special minutes together.

When we left the park, he said,

> Pots, we had a grandfather and grand-
> son picnic. It was the best ever.

I told him people enjoyed meeting him on our picnics,
and he replied,

> Yes, picnics. Where you can tell
> your name, and ask other
> people their names.

Katherine died in February of 2001, following a stroke. I had etched on her tombstone,

*"She gave her deep love,*
*and now she is at home in heaven."*

She surely gave Charlie her deepest love, profoundly making his life the better for it.

In January of 2003, Kristi and I were married at Christ Church Cathedral in Houston. Our families followed us out of the church, as Charlie, to the delight of all who saw, raised his clasped hands in triumph. Sometime later, before Mother's Day, Charlie told Kristi he had a surprise for her. Gently grasping her shoulders and looking into her eyes, he said,

Happy Mother's Day, Kristi.

~

Writing about his class visit to a Mexican restaurant, he wrote,

I raised my milk up and said,
'Cheers!' for everyone that went
to the Mexican restaurant today.

At our fitness center the manager and some members of
her staff were in the midst of a heated discussion which they
couldn't seem to resolve. Charlie walked in, and was asked by
the manager, "What can you suggest to keep us all from
arguing with each other…how can we get along better?"
He thought for a few minutes and replied,

**" Sleep a lot. "**

She asked for any further ideas, so he slowly added,

**" Do not let things bother you. "**

Followed by,

**" Whistle! "**

By that time they were all smiling. She later wrote us,

*How blessed we are for this Fitness Center angel, who came recently in
my office and, in a few short moments, taught the four of us that the
answers we seek are really not that complicated after all. Thanks to
Melinda (aka mom) for letting us spend an hour with Charlie every
Wednesday. He is, indeed, our weekly blessing.*

Should you go to that fitness center, you would easily know
where to find Charlie. Just look at the television monitors in
front of the treadmills. Next to the business and world news,

and perhaps a cooking class, you'll see the screen that's constantly tuned to the Cartoon Network.

I asked Charlie where his suggestion to

"Whistle!"

came from, and he told me,

"Pots, you know don't you, from *The Berenstain Bears* by Stan and Jan Berenstain. You remember when Sister Bear and Brother Bear were making too much noise. They wouldn't stop arguing. So Mama Bear whistled as loud as she could, and they stopped. You remember that, don't you?"

When Jan Berenstain died, Charlie emailed Stan, whom he didn't know, telling him how much he enjoyed the books and how sad he was to hear Jan had died. Stan replied, thanking him for his words.

~

On a family trip Melinda fell down a large step. Seeing she was hurt, Charlie said,

"Mom, I want to go to a church to say a prayer for you."

I think of Charlie's praying, and it brings me smiles.

It brings all of us smiles. I will share this with you. Every time
he eats macaroni and cheese, he puts his hands together,
bows his head, has the whole family do the same, and recites
a special prayer he learned from the movie *Home Alone.*

> **Bless this highly nutritious,
> micro-wavable, macaroni and
> cheese dinner, and the people
> who sold it on sale.**

~

For years, Charlie and a classmate who I'll call Jane had an
earnest competition about who could be first in line, in any
line, in any classroom. Then they arrived in Connie's class,
who told them that another student was subject to terrible
seizures and would always need to be first. That's all it took.
The competition was over.

~

In a small field house on a quiet neighborhood street, the
Briarwood Mustangs and another team were playing basketball.
There were only a few benches along one wall, but the fans
didn't require much space. Just a few parents, grandparents
and friends. Charlie, now twenty, was the tallest, oldest and
most experienced team member, and also the captain.
His team won the game, and that pleased Charlie. But that's
not what I want to share with you. What deeply touched
Melinda and me was his thoughtfulness. While he scored his

share of points, he also made sure even the most inexperienced player on his team got the ball and had his or her chances to play. Here was an autistic young man who really wants to win, but who also really cares for others.

His mom and I both had to wipe away tears.

~

Remember when I told you about the first time he played basketball not by his scripted rules, but by the rules of basketball? What I didn't tell you was that he noticed a Downs youngster on the other team walk into the gym after the game had started. In the midst of his anxiety about his own playing, he left his team, walked up to the boy, and gave him a high five. I emailed Gary about it, and he responded, "What fun and how nice he is catching on to the new rules and playing with them so quickly. Also nice to hear that people are still more important than the game to Charlie. That is one guy who has his priorities straight."

He does have his priorities straight. He prompts me to reexamine my priorities. He inspires me to be a more thoughtful and considerate person.

CHARLIE LIKES HIMSELF. How profound that is.
With all of his limitations, of which I think he is somehow
aware, he likes himself. He can experience frustration and
sadness, and talk about it…and still he likes himself. At the
end of the day, he chooses to find his glass half full. He has
truly taken a sour lemon and chosen to add sugar to make
lemonade. His life is hard. His response is to work hard.
And to take great pride in his success.

Those of us around him are somehow made better. With all
of our disappointments and frustrations and sadness, we are
surprised to experience we like ourselves in ways we never
dreamed. We discover that we are inspired.

So here is Charlie, in his words. And here is when these words were shared with us. What treasured words they are:

I don't know what I would do without myself.

*I don't know what I would do without him.*

~

God gave me web toes, like a duck. That was nice of him.

*His response when I once asked how he was different.*

~

I am a very popular boy in class.

*After telling him she was sure that was true,*
*Melinda asked how he arrived at that.*
*He told her he had been asked to make up a sentence*
*using his spelling words.*

That means I am amiable and affable.

*After announcing to his teacher he was, at age eighteen,
an adult…and replying to her question whether
or not he knew what being an adult meant.*

~

Mom, I look so handsome
in my church sweater and my shoes.
Do you think Mrs. DeLaughter
will recognize me?

*Talking about his teacher
before leaving for school one morning.*

Pots, I have great news!
I won the election!
I was elected president
of the Student Council!

I was so patiently waiting,
and when they announced I had won
I did this...you know, two thumbs up.
I am so happy.

Sometimes you can call me Mr. President.
Sometimes you can call me
President Stubbs.

I may need a little bit of help,
But that's o.k.

I couldn't have done it without
all of my fans.

*On being elected president of the Student Council*
*of the Tuttle School, the Special School*
*at Briarwood*

Pots, I made me so proud!

*After playing one of his video games.*

~

Pots, I made me so happy!

*Later that day.*

~

Nothing is too big for me.

*After his teacher congratulated him on counting
the money from a school fair*

## Charlie Martin Stubbs

Delightful, Remarkable, Handsome
Who takes a deep breath when he is nervous
Who could teach a cooking class
Who feels happy
Who wants to visit Max and Whitney
Who loves to play with Annie
Who fears tornadoes & other dangerous things
because he doesn't want to die
Who misses Andrew
Who would like to work at Brookwood
Whose parents say he is really crafty
Who would like to improve on doing his best

Charlie Martin Stubbs

*Written in the fall of his sophomore year
of high school.*

In many ways we often don't think about, life is extraordinarily difficult for every special needs child or adult. That is also true for Charlie. And yet his spirit can soar. After successfully completing one of his video games, he leaned over to me,

> "Pots, I know it's hard. But the future's looking great for me."

~

Charlie. There he is. In his honesty, his innocence and—as another friend of mine says about all children and adults with special needs—his pureness.

Now, let's talk about you,
for whom I write:

How might you find your
Charlie, your Special One?

MY SINCERE HOPE IS THAT MY TELLING you about Charlie—and how I believe he saved me—will inspire you to find your Charlie, who I believe can change your life.

If you have a good life now, then I believe your Charlie can beautifully make it even better.

If you hurt, find an emptiness deep inside, feel part of you is hidden in the shadows, and might even say to yourself something in you dear and vital has died, then I believe your Charlie can save your life. And even rescue your soul.

Your Charlie…who needs you. Your Special One…whom you need.

I think of you and your Charlie. And I think of those who have lived tragic lives, and whose lives might have been saved had they found their Charlies.

You will find your own way to go about your search for your Charlie. It will mean much that it is your way, and I would enjoy knowing about your journey.

I have some thoughts that might be helpful for your journey.

~

Perhaps you might enjoy a story told several years ago by Vivian Shudde. Vivian is Yvonne Streit's daughter; she is now executive director of Brookwood and Yvonne is executive director emeritus. As Vivian and her daughter Sarah were driving home from school one day, Sarah told Vivian she was upset because certain parents she knew had decided not to have any more children beyond their two. Mind you, Sarah's aunt, Vicki, and her own brother, Wilson, both have special needs. Vivian explained some people have many children, some have none, and having two was just fine. Sarah replied, "But that means they will never have a special one." She continued, "I think I figured it out, mom. They just didn't pray hard enough."

Although I thought at the moment her words were dear, it took some time for me to capture their truth. While neither you nor I may ever have our own biological special needs child, I hope with everything in me that you, like me, will find in your life your own "Special One"—your own Charlie—and, like me with our Charlie, it will be your lucky day!

I have often wondered where I might find my Charlie, if I didn't already have him. The answer always brings me back to looking inside myself first, to exploring inside of me, and being open and honest with what I find. I know there was a time when what I found inside would have stood between me and Charlie.

Many years ago, Katherine and I, along with our three young children, Earle III, Grant and Melinda were walking down the street. I saw a mother and father and their young daughter turn onto our street walking towards us, the little girl in a wheelchair and fitted with stainless steel contraptions. Without hesitation I guided my family across the street, simply because I didn't want to look at her. She was different. She was hurt. I didn't want to face different and hurt, so I chose to look away.

I have thought again and again about my looking away. Not only that day, and not only from that little girl, but since then, on other days and from others with special needs. Is it simply being uncomfortable, and not knowing what to do? Is it a reluctance to be involved with someone who needs my help, and not knowing what would be asked of me? Could it be I might discover yet more of my inadequacies? Is it because I am afraid sadness and pain may be involved? I have wondered whether or not it is also because I have accepted without serious question the all too common practice of looking both down and away from these beautiful people as simply one of society's norms. At best a nice smile, perhaps a nod or a friendly pat on the head, and then on my way. Kind…but not caring. Have I even dared to tell myself I don't have the time?

I have accepted that for me there are uncomfortable truths in my answers to those questions, yet now I have become grateful for the discomfort, because thankfully I no longer look away. I found I could choose to overcome my reluctance, and as a result I have experienced joy really beyond description. I have discovered more of my inadequacies, and they are ample, but I have discovered I am needed and I have something to give. I have experienced pain and sadness, and that is not likely to be avoided, but I have also felt unexpected happiness and fulfillment and even just plain fun. As for not having the time, I have become more aware of the beauty found in the gift of time I share with Charlie. And I treasure that time.

I don't think your search will be that difficult. Deciding to begin your search, that is where I think the hard part lies. Because of my experience, I believe that before you begin looking for your Charlie, you must first look inside of you. You might be surprised at what you find. And, while it might feel uncomfortable to begin with, you might be glad to confront it, and be happy with the outcome.

After you find your Charlie, I believe you will discover that he or she will help you find the goodness inside yourself again if you have lost it, or show it to you, even if you have never believed it existed.

Forty years ago I served on the advisory board of an adoption agency, and one of our mothers gave birth to a little girl. She was born without a middle layer of skin, and we were told at puberty she would have "elephant man" skin. We agonized over where to place her, until one day a couple from a nearby small town arrived at our doorstep wanting to adopt a baby. The caseworker asked them what kind of baby they would like, and they replied, "We want a baby who needs us." That was all they wanted. We evaluated them, found them to be what we wanted in adoptive parents, and they went home with their new baby, both wanted and loved.

I will share with you a few suggestions of where you might look for your Charlie. The first thing is to look for someone who needs you.

~

Because Charlie has autism, I think your Charlie might have autism, too. But your Charlie could really have any special need.

I quote my dear friend again, "Each person with a special need is Special." Functionally disabled. Challenged. Developmentally delayed. Somehow brain damaged. They might be without a diagnosis or neglected or abused. So many hurt children and adults do their best in the face of immense challenges, and need someone who cares in their lives, someone who wants to share their lives.

It seems to me the first place to look for your Charlie is in your own home. If not there, perhaps in the home of someone in your family. For me it was Charlie's home. Often Charlies exist but are overlooked. I will always remember a couple I met who bought several copies of my book, *Dear Charlie*. When I asked them why they needed so many copies, they told me they had two autistic sons and they were hoping the books would encourage their own parents to become more involved with the boys.

~

Look next door, across the street, down the block. Look for someone whom you first might see as different, and from whom you might shy away. I think the key is to look, rather than looking away.

~

You might look into Special Olympics, that magnificent organization born out of the vision and hard work of Eunice Shriver. Explore their website and volunteer at some of their many events. Watch and help and perhaps come to know some of the awe-inspiring Special Olympians. Perhaps you will encounter someone like the Downs youngster outside of a track meet who came up to our frisky black Labrador retriever, rolled in delight on the ground with him, and, looking up, asked his name. We told him his name was Nimrod. We had named him after the first great hunter in the Bible, but we have discovered that to a younger generation the name means "dumb-dumb." After a thoughtful pause, with a wonderful and kind innocence he asked, "Can I rename him?"

And perhaps someday you might wear a ribbon which reads,

Volunteer
Special Olympics
Skill
Courage
Sharing
Joy

~

Another place you could look is the website for "Best Buddies," founded by Anthony Kennedy Shriver, "dedicated to establishing a global volunteer movement that creates opportunities for one-to-one friendships, integrated employment and leadership development for people with intellectual and developmental disabilities." On the website of "Best Buddies Texas" you will find the photograph of a smiling, winsome young high school boy, and next to his image the words, "I see you. As a classmate. As an equal. As a friend. Do you see me?" And, nearby, these words: "Get involved."

~

You might discover a residential community not that far away, a place you never knew existed. Perhaps it will be something like Brookwood, the community about twenty miles from Houston where men and women face the hard challenges which come with disabilities, and do so with grace, courage and success. It is a community where every room has an empty chair, God's chair, so that the citizens who live there know they are never alone. On a wall of its chapel, its truly Interfaith Worship Center, are these words from the fourth chapter of Isaiah:

> *But they that wait upon the Lord*
> *shall renew their strength;*
> *they shall mount up with wings as eagles;*
> *they shall run, and not be weary;*
> *and they shall walk, and not faint.*

I think of Charlie reading those words, and being inspired and encouraged by them. And I imagine he—and all the Charlies at Brookwood—will know God, in the special way a little child knows God.

You might join in the company of others whose lives are enriched by volunteering in such a place. And there you might find your Charlie.

Not long ago Charlie and I returned home from Brookwood, after a Special Olympics basketball game and dinner at their café, each of us with a carton of chicken salad. He told me,

" Pots, this has been a great day. An absolutely delightful day. A grandfather and grandson day, just like a father and son day. We have had a grandfather and grandson bonding day, just like my dad and I have a father and son bonding day. "

You might be surprised what you find in your community. It might be at a church or a particular caring organization. Two years ago I read this notice in the volunteer section of *The Houston Chronicle*:

> *Special needs children respond enthusiastically to the love and attention they get from caring adults in a program called Family Friends.*
>
> *Each volunteer is assigned a child to visit once a week for a one-on-one session of recreation and conversation. The time spent with these youngsters helps enrich their self-esteem and gives their parents a little time off to attend to other matters. Training for new volunteers will be held Tuesday and Wednesday.*

~

It might be a nearby camp, such as Camp For All, located in Texas near Houston. On its website it describes itself as "a unique camping and retreat facility that strives to enrich the lives of people with special needs." Another place might be one of the Hole in the Wall Camps founded by Paul Newman, "serving children and their families coping with cancer and other serious illnesses and conditions."

~

Look for people who have already found their Charlies, whose lives have been changed…and, in some instances, saved.

When you find them you will recognize them. They are people who have known tears but also laughter, who have been beautifully humbled but also raised to new heights. Because of them and their Charlies I think you will like them. Through them you may find your Charlie.

~

And your finding your Charlie may be accidental. Not by plan or design, but just by happening. Because you have opened yourself for it to happen. You have invited it to happen.

~

As you meet others who have found their Charlies, and even others who are involved in the life of your Charlie—other Charlie's Angels—I suggest you do all you can to learn from them. I believe what you learn will be personally meaningful, and will begin a dialogue in which you will share your thoughts and experiences with them and others.

~

In his book *Another Season,* Gene Stallings, who has been head football coach at Texas A&M and Alabama, tells about his son, John Mark, who had Downs Syndrome. He also had a serious heart condition, and this is what his dad wrote about one of John Mark's doctors.

> *If there was one other constant support during those years it was our new pediatric cardiologist, Dan McNamara, who had come highly recommended by our pediatrician....No doubt we had some good doctors, but many of them had sort of patted Johnny and said things like, "Oh, isn't he cute?" But from Dr. McNamara, we got true warmth....I sensed that Johnny was an individual to Dr. McNamara, a real valuable little person.*

Call it what you will: true warmth, treating one as an individual or respect. It is as important as anything you or I can do.

~

Recognize the esteem you will feel for your Charlie, and do all you can to help him or her develop more self esteem. It will be well grounded in him or her, and all you have to do is to give it voice and value.

You might find your Charlie already has a self esteem you would love to have. But you might find something else tucked in him or her as well—the scourges of shame, guilt, fault and inadequacy—inflicted by experiences with those who just don't understand, those who just don't get it. Thankfully you will understand, you will get it, and you can work to right any wrongs your Charlie has felt.

When we first realized Charlie was not "normal," when we
learned he had a pervasive developmental disorder, and when
we were later sure he had autism, we went through periods of
comparing him with other boys and girls. We asked over and
over, "What if…? And we said far too long, "If only…."
With guidance from those wiser than us, we gradually came
to see that comparing was a frustrating and useless exercise.
Better to see him as the treasured individual he is, and to
confine our comparisons to how he was doing in comparison
only to himself.

That is my suggestion when it comes to your Charlie, not
to compare him or her with anyone else, not to our Charlie
or anyone. Your Charlie is your treasure. Reserve your
comparisons to how he or she is doing in comparison only
to himself or herself.

~

Reflect on your entering into a world of little children,
perhaps not unlike the world of little children spoken of in
the Christian New Testament. Your Charlie will introduce you
to this new world, not literally of little children, but of pureness,
and love, and kindness and innocence. Walk with anticipation
and with care.

Be ready for frustrations, and discover that both you and your
Charlie can struggle to deal with them. Be ready for patience,
and learn that both you and your Charlie have more patience
than you thought. It is not going to be a conventional walk in

the park. Your park will have its rough places, its sadness and hurt, but you may find it to be a beautiful park.

I suggest you begin where you are. By that I mean start where you think you can begin. Accept what limits you feel are now in your life, and give what you feel you can appropriately give. Just be open to allowing your relationship with your Charlie to become what it might become.

~

I have shared with you some ideas about your search for your Charlie, about where you might look and some of my thoughts of how you might go about it.

~

# I hope you have already discovered in these pages a sense of what finding your Charlie can mean to you.

You may discover, as did I
with Charlie,
the life giving power
in simply being with
your Charlie.

You may become inspired,
perhaps having forgotten
the last time you
were inspired.

You may find your perspective,
long muddled and cluttered,
now made surprisingly
clear and welcome.

You may find a beautifully
and refreshingly
new meaning to the words
love
admiration
beauty
hero
blessing.

You may find
a best friend,
and discover what it means
to bond with him or her
and to protect him or her
and what an amazing gift that is.

You may find you are needed
in ways you never thought about;
you are important in ways
you never considered.

You may find something
deep within yourself,
perhaps your Charlie within
whom you never knew
or long ago forgot about.

You may find your life
profoundly changed
…and perhaps saved.

You may find your soul
has been touched
…and perhaps rescued.

There you have it.
How Charlie saved my life…
and rescued my soul.
How we searched for him,
and who we found him to be.
How you might have your life changed,
if not saved…
and how your soul might be rescued,
by your own Charlie.

And, before we part,
I will share my hopes
for the future:

for you, for me
and for Charlie

### FOR YOU...

I keep on a shelf in my study
an empty jellybean box
which Charlie gave me on Christmas day
of 1999.

At the time,
he said to me,

> "Pots, here is something
> to remember me by"

And I gave him "My Nanny's" music box,
which sits by his bed.

I give you this book to remember Charlie by,
and I ask you to treasure him
as I treasure him.

I hope you look for
your Charlie...
and treasure him or her.

I hope you rejoice
in
your changed life.

FOR ME...

When I was six years old, I lived in a house
my parents rented across the street from
where Kristi and I now live, the same
street on which Charlie lives.
I remember, as if it were yesterday, spending
hours by a tree in our front yard, watching
a butterfly emerge from a cocoon. I didn't
look for such things, but just happened to
notice it as I played nearby. I think of it
as one of the most inspiring experiences
of my life.

On my desk there is a Celtic Cross,
some fourteen inches high,
and of a mottled brown color.
It was made at the Brookwood Community,
where I hope Charlie will someday live.
I imagine Charlie might make such a Cross.
In its center, on an orange square,
is an etching of a butterfly.

I sit at my desk and I look at the
Cross and the butterfly. I think of Charlie,
and I smile. The butterfly will always be Charlie.
Like the butterfly emerging years ago, I reflect
on his emergence. I am inspired. I am changed.
My life is saved.
And my soul is rescued.

## AND FOR CHARLIE...

If you should ever read this book,

I hope you will begin
to understand
how much you mean
to your Mom and your Dad,
to Andrew and Max and Whitney,
to your Nanny and to Kristi
and to me.

I hope you will grasp
how much joy and wisdom
you have brought us all.
To all whom you have known
and to all who have known you.

Thank you for your love
and
for opening us up to
our better selves.

We love you.

Pots

# ACKNOWLEDGEMENTS

My heartfelt thanks to all those who have made this book possible.
To Charlie first of all, and then to all of those whom we call
"Charlie's Angels."

I have received invaluable help in the writing of the book.
Melinda and Sam, Charlie's mom and dad. Kristi, my wife and
Charlie's "new grandmother." Roxana Wieland, for her beautiful
watercolor on the cover and her illustrations. Lucy Chambers
and Ellen Cregan of Bright Sky Press, bringing to bear their
devotion and skill. Gary Mesibov, our touchstone in Charlie's life.
And Chris Woods, for his guidance and suggestions.

## CAST OF CHARACTERS

**Charlie's Angels**

Charlie takes great delight in the Cast of Characters
which appears at the end of his Nintendo games,
often playing them several times.

So I think it appropriate to include here
some of the members of the Cast of Characters
of his life. Those who have honored him and whom
he has honored. Those whom we call "Charlie's Angels."

This list cannot begin to be complete,
and I thank those other Charlie's Angels left unnamed.
I thank you and I believe you thank Charlie.

## CAST OF CHARACTERS, continued

### His Family

*Melinda and Sam Stubbs*
*Andrew, Max and Whitney Stubbs*
*Katherine Martin*
*Kristi and Earle Martin*
*Deborah and Earle Martin III*
*Tom, Daniel and Grant Martin*
*Grant Martin*
*Dotty and Jack Stubbs*
*Karen and Kenneth Stubbs*

### His Teachers

*Ashley DeLaughter*
*Christine Forrest*
*Doug Helzer*
*Connie Hooper*
*Irene Keay*
*Margaret Kroeger*
*Susan Rieke*
*Carol Selby*
*Jane Stewart*
*Carole Wills*

### More Charlie's Angels

*Deborah Bunn Alley*
*Cedar Baldridge*
*Ellen Cassin*
*Macy Cassin*
*Will Condon*
*Leonor Delgado*
*Mary Jane Edwards*
*Bruce Harrover*
*Celina Hellmund*
*Yolanda Herrera*
*Ellen Hill*
*Diana Knox*
*Patty and Mark Langdale*

*Stephanie and Jean Malo*
*Philip Malo*
*Cynthia and Tony Petrello*
*Carena Petrello*
*Vivian Shudde*
*Yvonne Streit*
*Patti Stanwood*
*Lindel Toussant*
*Carol Whitmore*

*and*

*Gary Mesibov*

# CITED REFERENCES

## Introduction

Page 4: Gary B. Mesibov, Lynn W. Adams, and Laura G. Klinger, *Autism: Understanding the Disorder* (New York: Plenum Press, 1997), 105.

Page 5: Temple Grandin, *Thinking in Pictures* (New York: Doubleday, 1995), 76. Reference: Joliffe, T., Lakesdown, R., and Robinson, C. 1992 Autism, a personal account. *Communication* 26, 3:12-19.

## In Search of Charlie

Page 10: Arnold Miller and Eileen Eller-Miller, *From Ritual to Repertoire* (New York: John Wiley & Sons, 1989).

Page 11: Susan J. Moreno, editor, *The MAAP* (Crown Point, Indiana: MAAP Services, Inc.)

Page 15: Earle P. Martin, Jr., *Dear Charlie, A Guide to Living Your Life with Autism* (Arlington, Texas: Future Horizons Inc., 1999). [Also on page 5 of *Finding Your Charlie*.]

## For You to Know Charlie

Page 15: Stan and Jan Berenstain, *The Berenstain Bears Get In A Fight* (New York: Random House, 1982).

## Finding Your Charlie

Page 10: Gene Stallings and Sally Cook, *Another Season, A Coach's Story of Raising an Exceptional Son* (New York: Little Brown and Company, 1997), 83.

## RESPONSES

*When a painful new awareness settled on his extended family that Charlie truly was—and would always be—different...they couldn't know that his diagnosis would eventually bond them in unimaginable ways. In* The Boy Who Saved My Life, *Earle Martin shares his love for his autistic grandson, and how his journey with Charlie helps him rediscover himself. Every family facing an unexpected difference in a loved one will benefit from Martin's insights.*

~ PATRICIA KILDAY HART,
*Houston Chronicle*

*While reading this book, I laughed, I cried and I reflected on the beauty that suffuses family love and closeness...Earle Martin is a wise man whose life experiences have been many and varied. His appreciation for Charlie's many gifts and sharing of Charlie's perspectives on life are just some of the treasures contained in this book.*

~ SUSAN J. MORENO,
*President of OASIS at MAAP/MAAP Services for Autism and Asperger's Syndrome*

*Whether you are just entering the world of autism or have been involved for many years,* The Boy Who Saved My Life, *presents the truth that though challenges lie ahead for everyone in the family, there also are opportunities for personal growth and expanded comprehension of a complex and sometimes frightening realm. By sharing his relationship with his grandson, Earle Martin shows all of us that a diagnosis of autism—or any condition—does not have to mean a lifetime of loneliness and fear. Ultimately, life becomes what we make of it...whether we have autism or not.*

~ MARGARET LARSEN,
*President/CEO, Special Olympics Texas*

*Such a wonderful example of what happens to us when we turn away from ourselves and the pitfalls into which we are heading in order to help someone else. Exiting that trap turns into a win/win situation. Charlie brings to light another world for us to experience, another adventure to explore and enjoy the unforeseen beautiful surprises that come from walking side by side with another life. To look at things from a different perspective is an opportunity given to few. What a joy to experience these things from reading this book.*

~ YVONNE STREIT,
*Founder and Executive Director Emeritus of The Brookwood Community*

The text in *The Boy Who Saved My Life* is set in two typefaces.
The words of Earle, the narrator, for whom language comes
easily, are set in New Baskerville. Designed in 1757 by
John Baskerville, this transitional typeface resulted from
Baskerville's intent to improve upon the types of William
Caslon. The resulting simplicity and quiet refinement reflect
Baskerville's ideals of perfection. The words of Charlie,
which are very precious to those who love him and which
for many years seemed like a miracle, are set in Helvetica
Neue. Redesigned from the 1957 classic Helvetica in 1983,
Helvetica Neue overcomes the limitations of the original
typeface, allowing total design freedom. The refinements
resulted in improved legibility and usefulness.

The inks are green and charcoal grey to reflect the beauty
that can be found in the shadows and the ability of friendship and love to create growth.

The illustrations were created by Roxana Wieland from
original photographs of Charlie. An artist who specializes in
watercolor, mainly portraits, her paintings reside in private
collections throughout the United States. She resides in
Northern Michigan. For commissioned portraits, she can be
reached at roxanawieland@hotmail.com.